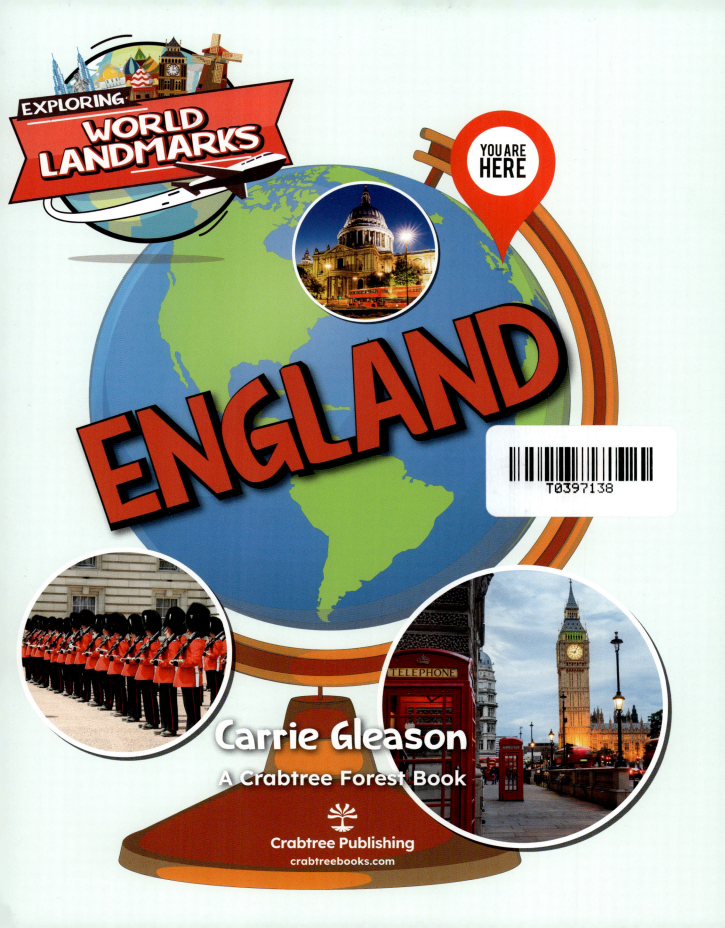

Developed and produced by Plan B Book Packagers
www.planbbookpackagers.com
Art director: Rosie Gowsell Pattison
Author: Carrie Gleason
Crabtree editor: Ellen Rodger
Prepress technician: Margaret Salter
Production coordinator: Katherine Berti
Proofreader: Crystal Sikkens
Photographs:
All images from Shutterstock.com

Crabtree Publishing

crabtreebooks.com   800-387-7650
Copyright © 2024 Crabtree Publishing
All rights reserved. No part of this publication may be reproduced, stored in a retrieval system or be transmitted in any form or by any means, electronic, mechanical, photocopying, recording, or otherwise, without the prior written permission of Crabtree Publishing.

Hardcover   978-1-0398-1538-4
Paperback   978-1-0398-1564-3
Ebook (pdf) 978-1-0398-1616-9
Epub   978-1-0398-1590-2

Published in Canada
Crabtree Publishing
616 Welland Avenue
St. Catharines, Ontario
L2M 5V6

Published in the United States
Crabtree Publishing
347 Fifth Avenue
Suite 1402-145
New York, NY 10016

Library and Archives Canada Cataloguing in Publication
Available at the Library and Archives Canada

Library of Congress Cataloging-in-Publication Data
Available at the Library of Congress

Printed in the U.S.A./072023/CG20230214

Contents

Next Stop: England! .... page 4

Big Ben .... page 6

Stonehenge ....page 8

Buckingham Palace .... page 10

The London Eye .... page 12

White Cliffs of Dover .... page 14

Tower of London .... page 16

London Zoo .... page 18

Salisbury Cathedral .... page 20

Lake District .... page 22

Warwick Castle .... page 24

Uffington White Horse .... page 26

Trafalgar Square .... page 28

Kew Gardens .... page 30

Hadrian's Wall .... page 32

221B Baker Street .... page 34

Royal Observatory .... page 36

Sherwood Forest .... page 38

Eden Project .... page 40

Angel of the North .... page 42

Tower Bridge .... page 44

England at a Glance .... page 46

Glossary .... page 47

Learning More .... page 48

Index .... page 48

Next Stop: England!

Welcome to England! England's landmarks are some of the best known around the world. It is a country of royal palaces and castles, ancient and pop culture spots, and beautiful countryside and coasts.

FIVE England Facts

1. England has a monarch, or king or queen, as its head of state. The role of monarch is hereditary. Relatives of the monarch are called the royal family.

2. England is one country that makes up the United Kingdom. The others are Wales, Northern Ireland, and Scotland. UK citizens are called British. People who live in England are called English.

3. England's geography is mostly low hills and plains, with some mountains in the north. It also has many sea coasts.

4. England's weather is mainly cloudy days, rain, and fog.

5. England has been invaded several times in its history. Invaders included Romans (from Italy), Anglo-Saxons (from Germany), Vikings, and Normans (from France).

WHAT IS A LANDMARK?

Landmarks are unique natural or human-made structures that tell us where in the world we are. In your neighborhood, a landmark might be a large tree in the center of town, a special building, or a park. Countries also have landmarks, but on a much bigger scale. Examples of landmarks might be large mountains and waterfalls, ancient buildings and statues, and modern bridges and towers.

Eden Project

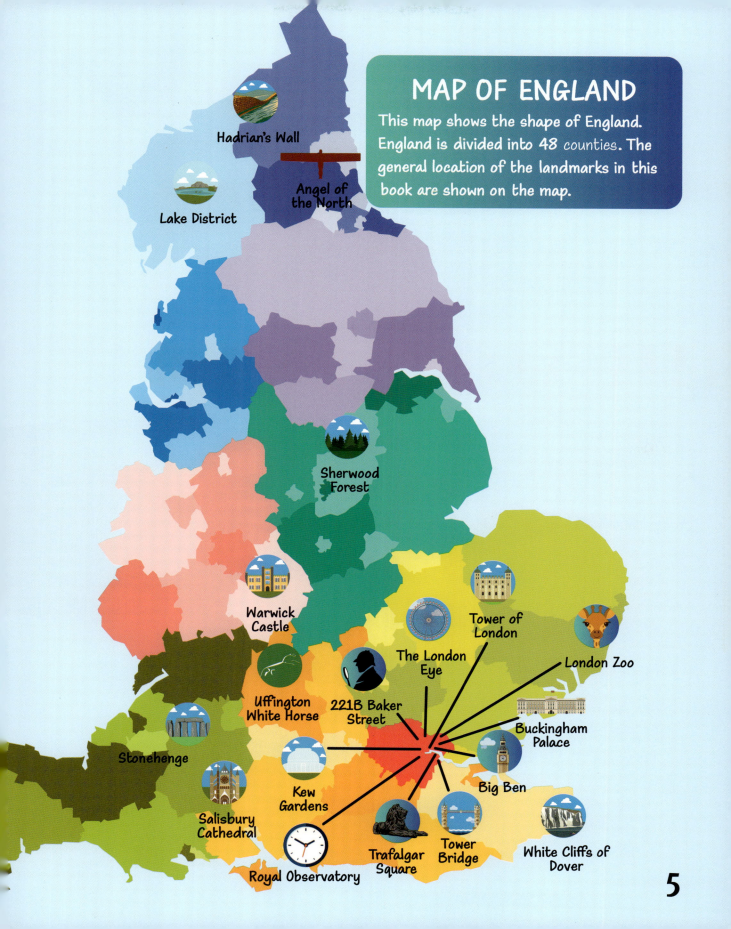

Big Ben

Every hour, Big Ben can be heard echoing across London—England's capital and biggest city. Big Ben is the name of the largest bell in the Elizabeth Tower, but the tower itself is also often called Big Ben. The clock tower was built in 1859 and is attached to Westminster Palace, the home of the British parliament. The tower, with its four clock faces, is England's most famous landmark. There are four smaller bells inside the tower's belfry, the part of a clock tower where bells are rung. They chime a tune called "Westminster Quarters" every 15 minutes, while Big Ben's deeper gongs signal the hour of the day.

One of the features of the clock tower is the Ayrton Light, which is lit at night. It was originally installed in 1885 by order of Queen Victoria. It was shone at Buckingham Palace so the queen could see if parliament was working at night. The British queen or king is not allowed inside the House of Commons, where decisions about how the United Kingdom is run take place!

Stonehenge

Stonehenge is one of the greatest mysteries of ancient England. No one knows who arranged these large, heavy stones in a circle, or why. Archaeologists think that construction of the site began about 5,000 years ago and it was added to in different stages over time. They have discovered that the site contains the remains of dead bodies, leading some to believe that Stonehenge was used as a place for burials and ceremonies. There have been other, more bizarre ideas about Stonehenge over the years, including that it was built by the wizard Merlin or by aliens. In the 1600s, one English duke even dug a hole in its center, hoping to find buried treasure!

(background) One theory about Stonehenge is that it was created as an ancient calendar. The largest stones line up perfectly with the sunrise on the longest day of the year (called the summer solstice), and the sunset on the shortest day of the year (the winter solstice). People still gather at Stonehenge today to celebrate the solstices.

8

(left) Other ancient stone "henges," or circles, are dotted across the country. Stonehenge (shown here from above) is the most famous.

9

Buckingham Palace

Buckingham Palace is the official London home of England's ruling monarch. It is the country's most famous palace. Palaces are very grand, very showy homes built for kings and queens and members of the royal family. Buckingham Palace is just one of several royal palaces in England. It is owned by a corporation called the Crown Estate and is not the personal property of the king. Buckingham Palace is said to be the most expensive home in the world.

(background) Buckingham Palace is huge! It has 52 bedrooms, 78 bathrooms, and 19 state rooms where ceremonies take place. It also has 188 rooms for staff, 92 offices, a swimming pool, a cinema, and a health clinic. As many as 800 people work in the palace at one time. But despite all its fanciness, it is also home to a large population of rats!

(above) Four times a week, a ceremony called the Changing of the Guards takes place in front of the palace.

The London Eye

The London Eye is an enormous observation wheel that opened in the year 2000 to mark the beginning of the new millennium. It looks like a giant bicycle wheel suspended over the Thames River, England's longest river. The wheel has 32 egg-shaped capsules, or pods, attached to it. Here, riders can get a bird's-eye view of the city of London. It takes 30 minutes for the wheel to make one full rotation, or trip from start to finish.

(left) When it was built, the London Eye was the highest place from which to look over London. But when the building called the Shard was built in 2013, it included an even higher observation deck.

(background) The London Eye was challenging to build because it was put together over the Thames River. Pieces of the wheel were shipped up the river on barges and then lifted up in sections using a floating crane.

White Cliffs of Dover

The White Cliffs of Dover is recognized around the world as the most famous coastline in England. The white cliffs are made of chalky white rock called limestone. Millions of years ago, England was buried beneath the sea, and the remains of tiny sea plants called coccoliths built up over time to form rock. When the rock later rose out of the ocean, it formed the White Cliffs of Dover.

From a distance, the White Cliffs of Dover look like they have been coated with white paint and topped by a green roof. They are a symbol of home for people returning to England from France and can be seen for many miles across the narrowest part of the English Channel. The channel separates England from the European mainland.

15

Tower of London

The Tower of London is a castle built by William the Conqueror in the 1070s. William the Conqueror led the Norman Invasion of England in 1066. He declared himself king and built many castles in England to protect his kingdom, including the Tower of London. The tower is known for its tall, defensive walls and at one time had a moat around it! Over the years, the castle was used as a home for royalty, to store England's money and royal valuables, as a zoo, and as a prison. It is said to be the most secure place in London and is guarded by Yeomen Warders, who still live within its walls with their families today. One Yeomen Warder is called the Ravenmaster, whose job it is to care for seven ravens. According to superstition, if the ravens leave, the tower and the kingdom will fall.

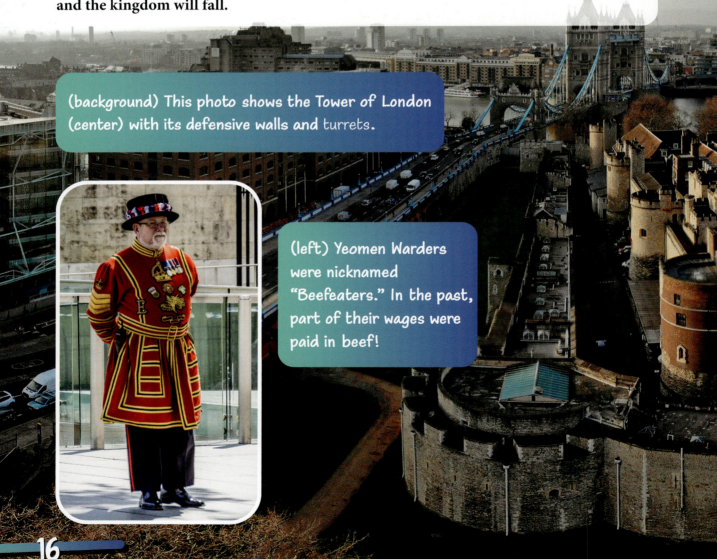

(background) This photo shows the Tower of London (center) with its defensive walls and turrets.

(left) Yeomen Warders were nicknamed "Beefeaters." In the past, part of their wages were paid in beef!

FIVE Famous Tower Prisoners

1 Scottish knight William Wallace, who fought for independence from England. Drawn and quartered in 1305.

2 Two young princes imprisoned in 1483 by their uncle, who wanted to be king. The princes were never seen again!

3 Anne Boleyn, second wife of King Henry VIII, for treason. Beheaded in 1536.

4 Explorer Sir Walter Raleigh, imprisoned in the "Bloody Tower" for plotting against the king in 1603.

5 Soldier Guy Fawkes, imprisoned and tortured for plotting to bomb parliament in 1605.

17

London Zoo

The London Zoo is the world's oldest scientific zoo. It was created in 1828 for scientists to study animals. For its first 20 years, only members of the Zoological Society of London could visit it. Today it is open to the public. Through its history, famous zoo animals have included a gorilla named Guy, an elephant named Jumbo, and a black bear named Winnie that was the inspiration for the children's storybook character Winnie-the-Pooh. There have been a number of famous animal escapes at the zoo, too! A red panda, an eagle, a chimp, and a gorilla have all escaped their enclosures. During the bombing of London by enemy German planes in World War II (WWII)(1939–45), a zebra escaped when the Zebra House was damaged.

(background) Giraffes live at the zoo's Giraffe House, one of the oldest buildings at the zoo. When giraffes first arrived in London in 1836, zookeepers walked them down the streets from the port to the zoo. It was the first time people in London had seen a giraffe.

(above) The world's first Reptile House was built at London Zoo. The zoo also created the first public aquarium and insect house.

19

Salisbury Cathedral

In the middle ages, the period of England's history between 1066 and 1485, the Christian Church was an important part of people's lives. The Church was rich and powerful, and grand cathedrals were built as places of worship. It took decades to build the largest cathedrals. Hundreds of people were needed to lay the stone and create the stained glass windows and statues inside. The largest English cathedral is Salisbury Cathedral, in southwest England. It was built between 1220 and 1258. The cathedral also has one of the last original copies of England's most important document inside it, the Magna Carta. The Magna Carta was signed by King John I in 1215 and says that the king is not above the law.

(background) Salisbury Cathedral's spire (tip) is 405 feet (123 m) tall.

THREE Famous Churches

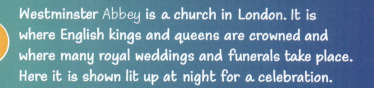

1. Westminster Abbey is a church in London. It is where English kings and queens are crowned and where many royal weddings and funerals take place. Here it is shown lit up at night for a celebration.

2. St Paul's Cathedral in London is known for its domed roof. The dome was built in 1675 after the cathedral was destroyed by a great fire in the city. Prior to this, it had also been destroyed by a fire in 675 C.E. and a Viking attack in 962 C.E.!

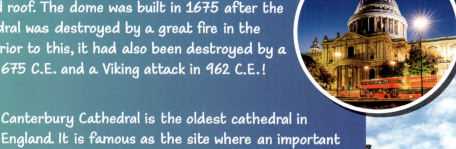

3. Canterbury Cathedral is the oldest cathedral in England. It is famous as the site where an important church leader was murdered by order of the king for arguing about the authority of the church in 1170. At the time, the Church and the state worked together to rule England, but arguments about power took place.

21

Lake District

England's Lake District is a popular spot for holidays. Its beautiful scenery has been an inspiration for many English poets, writers, and painters. The Lake District is located in England's northwest. The country's highest mountains, called fells, are found here, as well as long, narrow lakes and smaller ponds called tarns. The countryside was formed by geological processes millions of years ago. The rock is a type of volcanic rock, created when now extinct volcanoes erupted long ago. Later, glaciers swept across the land, carving out its many valleys and lakes.

(background) Lake District National Park was created in 1951 to preserve nature in the region. Heather, also called ling, is one of the most common plants that grow in the Lake District. When the flowers bloom in late summer, they blanket the hills in shades of pink and purple.

(left) Open areas of land are called moors. Bogs are swampy moors.

(right) The Lake District is an important habitat for birds and is a popular spot for birdwatching.

23

Warwick Castle

More than 4,000 castles were built all over England in the middle ages. A castle is a large structure built for defense, like a fort. They have walls around them and towers for guards. They were also the homes of kings, queens, and nobles, people who had been granted land and titles for being loyal to the king. Important people lived in a tower called a keep. It was the largest and safest part of the castle in case of an attack. Many castles are in ruins today. But some, such as Warwick Castle in central England, have been restored and are historical sites where people can see what it was like to live in them long ago.

(background) Warwick castle was built on a hill overlooking water, which provided additional defense.

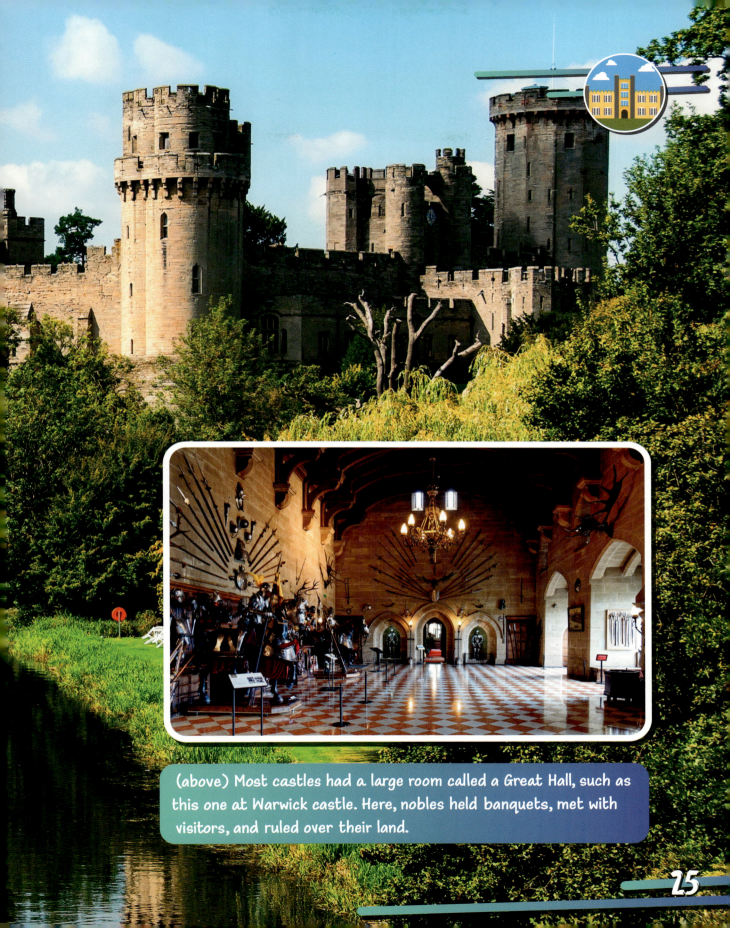

(above) Most castles had a large room called a Great Hall, such as this one at Warwick castle. Here, nobles held banquets, met with visitors, and ruled over their land.

Uffington White Horse

The Uffington White Horse is a giant "hill figure" carved into a hillside in southern England. It is believed to have been created by Celtic peoples more than 3,000 years ago. No one knows for sure why it was made, but it has been carefully maintained for thousands of years and is the oldest of several hill figures in the south. To make it, trenches were dug into the hillside in the shape of the horse, exposing the white, chalky limestone rock beneath. Other hill figures have been created since. It is likely that many once decorated the landscape of southern England, but were covered up by grass over time.

(background) The Celts were an ancient people who migrated from other parts of Europe to England thousands of years ago. The horse hill figure may have been based on their beliefs in gods and goddesses represented by horses.

26

(above) The Long Man of Wilmington is another hill figure in southern England. Like other hill figures, the reason why it was made, and by whom, is a mystery. Historians think the Long Man is much more recent than the White Horse, and was made in the 1700s.

27

Trafalgar Square

Trafalgar Square is a public gathering place in London. It was named after a famous naval battle fought against France and Spain in 1805 off the coast of Cape Trafalgar, Spain. Sculptures and monuments in the square honor England's great naval past. A strong navy helped England become a powerful empire. It allowed Britain to protect its island home from invaders and to travel the globe in search of new lands and trade goods. When British sailors landed in new places, they often declared those lands for themselves (even though there were people living there already!) This created the wealthy and powerful British Empire, with its headquarters in England. At its peak in 1922, the empire controlled almost 25 percent of the land on Earth.

(background) The tall column in Trafalgar Square was built to honor naval commander Horatio Nelson (Lord Nelson), who led the Battle of Trafalgar.

(above) The four Landseer lions lie at the base of Nelson's Column. They were made from the bronze cannons of the French and Spanish ships defeated at the Battle of Trafalgar.

(right) The HMS Victory was Lord Nelson's ship in the Battle of Trafalgar. By the 1700s, the British Empire ruled the seas with its navy. Many battles at sea have been won by its navy, which remained the world's most powerful until WWII.

Kew Gardens

Kew Gardens is the world's largest botanical garden. It is located on a 300 acre (121 hectare) property outside of London. The gardens here contain the world's largest collection of living plants. It also has 40,000 different kinds of seeds, and over 1 million different types of fungus. It is an important scientific research center for preserving plant biodiversity around the world. Scientists at Kew work with different countries to help save their native plants from extinction by establishing seed banks, where seeds are stored. The scientific center also houses collections from botanists, or scientists who study plants, who traveled the world with England's explorers long ago.

(background) A special feature of Kew Gardens is the enormous Victorian glasshouse in which plants from around the world are grown.

(above) A spiral staircase inside the gardens at Kew.

31

Hadrian's Wall

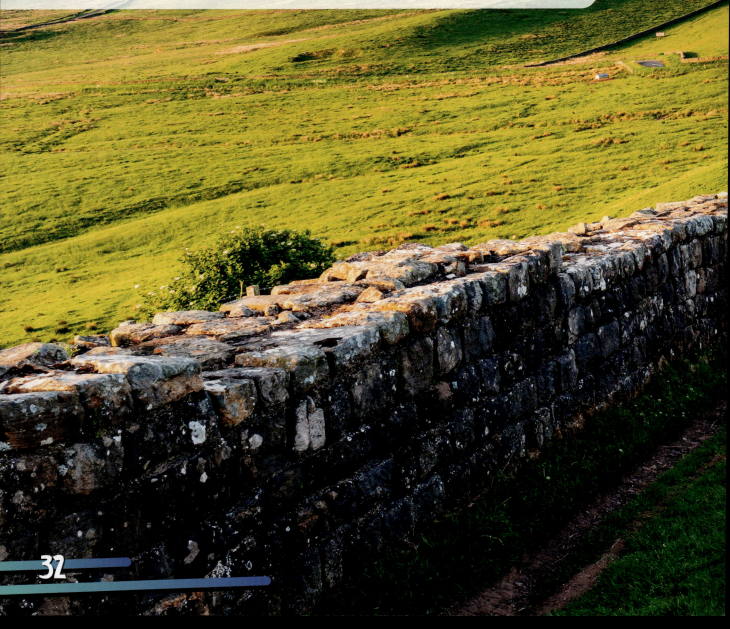

Hadrian's Wall is an ancient landmark in the north of England. It is the remains of a stone wall built in 122 C.E. by a Roman emperor named Hadrian. At the time, England had been invaded by the Romans and were ruled by them. The wall was built both to defend Roman England from invaders to the north, and to keep people under Roman rule from leaving! A series of forts and turrets were built along the wall, where soldiers stayed and worked, but no longer stand today. After Roman rule of England ended in 410 C.E., the country was broken up into several independent kingdoms.

When it was built, Hadrian's Wall was 15 feet (4.6 m) tall and stretched for 73 miles (117 km) from coast to coast across northern England. During Roman rule, roads, towns, sanitation, and public pools, called baths, were introduced to England.

221B Baker Street

(background) The black door on the left leads to Sherlock Holmes's fictional home.

34

The address 221B Baker Street, London, was made famous by British writer Sir Arthur Conan Doyle. Doyle chose the address as the home of his popular detective character Sherlock Holmes. The address 221B Baker Street did not exist when the first Sherlock Holmes story, "A Study in Scarlet," was published in 1887. The building numbers only went up to 100. Today 221B Baker Street is the Sherlock Holmes Museum, were fans can visit an apartment, called a "flat," done up to look like Holmes's in the books. However, even this 221B Baker Street is fictional—its actual street address is number 239!

THREE Pop Culture Spots

1 Abbey Road is a street in London. Its crosswalk was made famous after being used as artwork on the cover of an album by the Beatles, a band from Liverpool, in the northwest.

2 King's Cross Station is a railway station in central London. It is the setting for the fictional Platform 9¾ that student wizards in the Harry Potter books used to catch the train to Hogwarts.

3 Tardis is a time machine in the popular British sci-fi show Doctor Who. Tardis was based on police boxes that used to line streets in England, where police could call the station before there were cell phones.

Royal Observatory

The Royal Observatory in Greenwich, London, can be thought of as the place where time began. Here, an imaginary line running north-south from the poles through Greenwich was established in 1851. Its name is the prime meridian and represents zero degrees longitude on maps. It allowed **astronomers** to create accurate maps of the sky, which helped sailors navigate at sea. At the prime meridian, standardized time could also be kept. At first, Greenwich Mean Time meant that the day started at noon, when the sun was directly overhead of the prime meridian. Before this, every town and city kept their own time, which made it difficult to schedule trains. Everywhere in the world now uses a system of time based on Greenwich Mean Time, now called Universal Time.

(left) The prime meridian separates the globe into the east and west hemispheres.

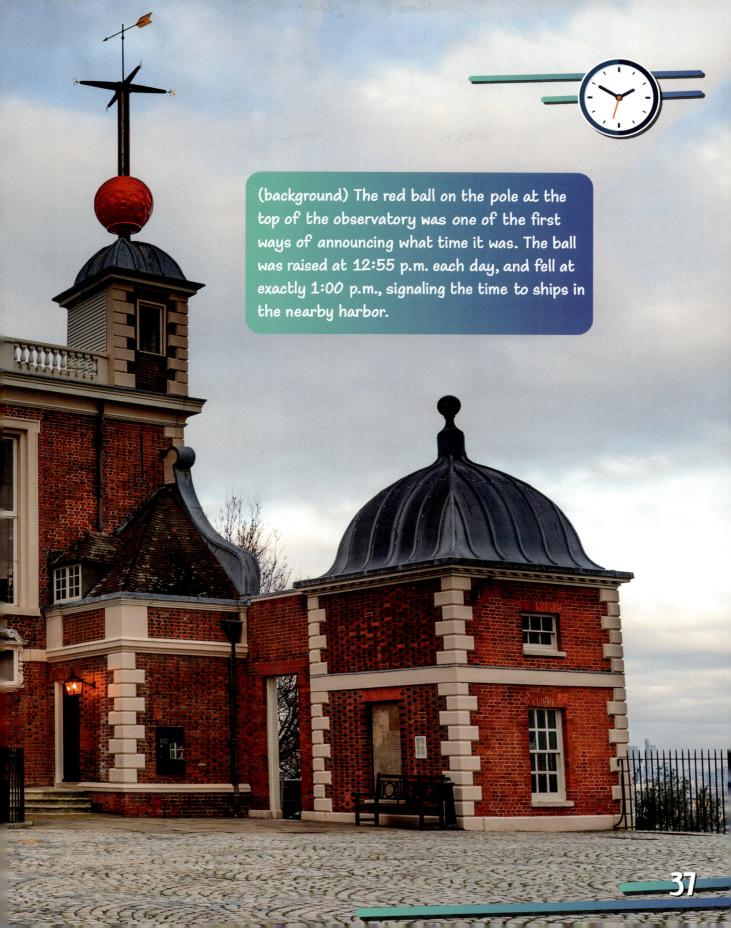

(background) The red ball on the pole at the top of the observatory was one of the first ways of announcing what time it was. The ball was raised at 12:55 p.m. each day, and fell at exactly 1:00 p.m., signaling the time to ships in the nearby harbor.

Sherwood Forest

Sherwood Forest in central England was once a Royal Hunting Forest, an area where only members of the royal family and the upper class, called the nobility, were allowed to hunt. It is also the home of the popular folk hero Robin Hood. In legends, Robin Hood is known for outsmarting powerful people and stealing from them to give to the poor. For much of its past, English society was strictly divided by class, or standing. Most people were "commoners," or poor workers who did not come from royal families. They had no land of their own, and no say in the ruling of the country. Robin Hood is a symbol of rebellion against England's powerful, wealthy ruling class.

(background) This tree in Sherwood Forest is named the Major Oak. It is claimed to have been the hideout of the outlaw Robin Hood and his band of Merry Men. The tree is thought to be the largest oak tree in England, and may actually be two or more trees that have grown into one.

(left) This statue of Robin Hood stands in front of Nottingham Castle, near Sherwood Forest. Robin Hood's arrow points at the castle entrance. Historians think that Robin Hood was not based on one real-life person, but a collection of different outlaws from the past.

Eden Project

The Eden Project was built inside an abandoned clay quarry, or pit, in southwest England. It was created to teach people about the environment and humans' interaction with plants. The main structures look like large bubbles. Here, thousands of plants from different parts of the world grow. There are two separate artificial biomes in the bubbles, one that is kept warm and moist like a rainforest to grow banana trees, coffee plants, giant bamboo, and other tropical plants. The other bubble mimics a Mediterranean biome, where plants like olive trees and grapes are grown. Outside is a garden where plants and flowers native to the English climate grow. The biomes are powered using energy from nearby wind turbines, and water for the plants comes from rainwater that collects in the quarry.

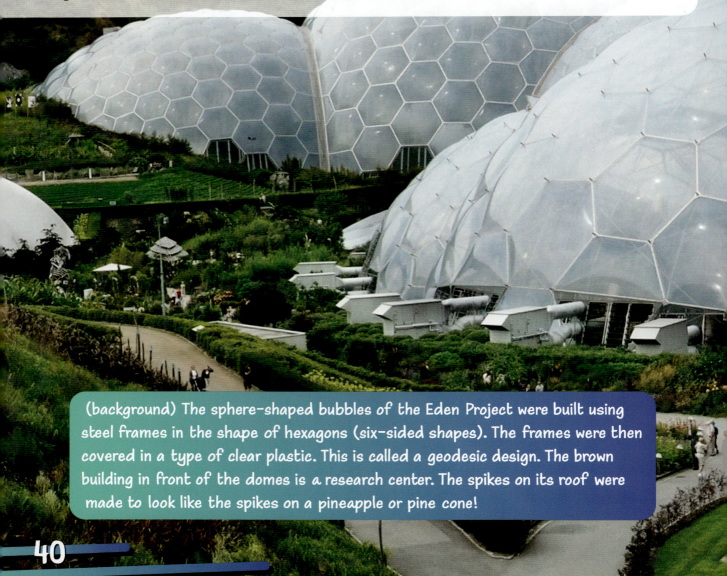

(background) The sphere-shaped bubbles of the Eden Project were built using steel frames in the shape of hexagons (six-sided shapes). The frames were then covered in a type of clear plastic. This is called a geodesic design. The brown building in front of the domes is a research center. The spikes on its roof were made to look like the spikes on a pineapple or pine cone!

(right) Sculptures can be found all over the Eden Project. This one in the Outdoor Gardens is called "Eve." It is made from clay, mirrors (on the face), and plants for hair.

(left) Pathways for visitors to look at the plants wind through the domes. In this picture you can see the steel frames of the geodesic roof.

Angel of the North

The Angel of the North is 65 feet (20 m) tall. It is made from weathering steel, which gives it a rusty look.

The Angel of the North is a statue in northeast England that sits on top of a former coal mine. Although the statue is modern, it is a symbol of northern England's industrial past, in particular its coal miners. A lot of coal was needed beginning in the mid-1700s to power England's Industrial Revolution, a period when many factories were built to make goods. Coal was used to power factories, as well as homes, ships, and trains. The coal was dug out from under Earth's surface by miners. It was hard, dirty, and dangerous work. The Angel of the North stands as a reminder of the area's coal miners and their contribution to northern England's industrial past. It is also a symbol of the region's transition to a new era.

Tower Bridge

Of the 35 bridges that span the Thames River in London, the Tower Bridge is the best known. It was designed to look like the Tower of London, located on the riverbank at the bridge's north end. Tower Bridge is a bascule bridge, which means it can be lifted in the center using counterweights to let ships pass. It works kind of like a seesaw. The counterweights are below the bridge, hidden from view by the tall towers on each side. Higher up, a glass-covered walkway runs between the towers. From the walkway, pedestrians get a view of the city, or look down and see the traffic on the road below through the walkway's glass floor!

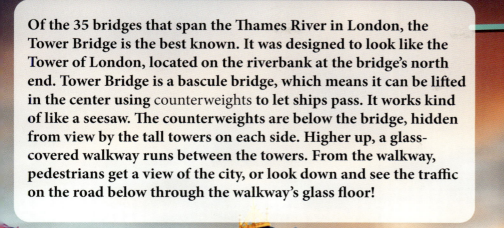

When Tower Bridge was completed in 1894, London was an important port for trading ships bringing goods from England's colonies. The bridge was lifted 20 to 30 times a day to allow large trading ships to enter London's ports. Today it is only raised once or twice a day for large sailboats.

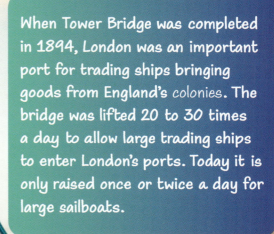

England at a Glance

Official Name .... England
Population 55,977,178
National Animal .... Barbary lion
Currency .... Pound sterling
Main Language .... English
Size .... 50,300 square miles
.... (130,280 square km)

Flag of England

Flag of the United Kingdom

England is a country on the island of Great Britain in the northwest Atlantic Ocean. This world map has the continents labeled and England highlighted in red.

Flight time from New York to England: Approximately 6.5 hours.

YOU ARE HERE

North America
South America
Europe
Africa
Asia
Australia

England has one time zone, called Greenwich Mean Time. In the summer, the clocks are set ahead by one hour to follow British Summer Time. This is like daylight savings time in North America.

Glossary

abbey A place where monks and nuns live and work.
archaeologist Someone who studies ancient humans' past.
astronomer A scientist who studies objects in space, such as the planets and stars.
barge A large, flat-bottomed boat.
biodiversity A great number of different living things.
biomes Regions of the world with similar climates, animals, and plants.
botanical A word to describe something to do with plants.
Christian Church The religious community of all Christians, or followers of the teachings of Jesus Christ.
coal A kind of dark-colored rock burned for fuel.
colony A land under control of another country.
corporation A type of organization run by a group of people.
counterweight A balancing, or equal weight.
county An administrative region in England, formerly called a "shire."
drawn and quartered A gruesome form of execution in which someone was hanged and then chopped into four pieces.
duke A noble title.
empire A ruling country and all the lands under its control.
extinction No longer in existence, or being.
folk Something that reflects the culture of common people.
geological Relating to the study of the surface of Earth and what it is made of.
glaciers Large, slow-moving rivers of ice.
head of state The highest-ranking person of a country.
hereditary Passed down from one generation to the next.

House of Commons The place where elected members of the government meet to discuss new laws and the issues of a country.
Industrial Revolution A movement away from goods being made by craftspeople to factories.
inspiration Being moved to do something creative.
invade To enter a country using force.
knight A type of soldier on horseback in the middle ages.
Mediterranean The area around the Mediterranean Sea, which lies between Europe, North Africa, and Western Asia.
migrate To move from one place to another.
millennium A period of 1,000 years.
native Belonging to a certain place.
naval A word to describe something to do with the navy.
parliament The legislative, or law-making, branch of the UK government.
pop culture The popular trends of a generation.
quarry A large, deep pit used for mining.
rebellion An uprising against a government.
sanitation Things related to public health such as clean drinking water and sewers.
title A name that shows position or rank.
treason The crime of betraying one's own country or government.
turret A tower on top of a larger tower, or at the corners of a castle.
Victorian A word that describes something from the time of Queen Victoria (1837–1901).
wind turbine A structure with blades that generate power from the wind's energy.
World War II (WWII) An international conflict between 1935 and 1945 that involved more than 50 countries.
worship To show honor or respect.

Learning More

Books

Amazing Landmarks: Discover the hidden stories behind 10 iconic structures! by Rekha S. Rajan. Scholastic Inc., 2022.

Your Passport to England (World Passport series) by Nancy Dickmann. Capstone Press, 2022.

England (Country Profiles series) by Amy Rechner. Blastoff! Discovery, 2017.

Websites

Britannica Kids: Visit the Landmarks article to learn about landmarks around the world.
https://kids.britannica.com/kids/article/landmarks-at-a-glance/608620

National Geographic Kids Countries Guides: Find out more about England and the United Kingdom.
www.kids.nationalgeographic.com/geography/countries/article/united-kingdom

Globe Trottin' Kids: Country information for kids.
www.globetrottinkids.com/countries/united-kingdom

Index

animals 10, 16, 18-19, 23, 46

Beatles, The 35
bogs 23

castles 4, 16-17, 24-25, 39, 45
Celts 26
churches 20-21

Doctor Who 35

English Channel 15
empire 28-29, 45
explorers 17, 30

guards 11, 16

Harry Potter 35
hill figures 26-27

kings 4, 7, 10, 16, 17, 20, 21

London 6-7, 8-9, 10-11, 12-13, 16-17, 18-19, 34-35, 28-29, 30-31, 36-37, 44-45

Magna Carta 20
mining 40, 43
mountains 4, 22

national parks 22
nobles/nobility 8, 24, 25, 38

observation platforms/ wheels 12-13, 45

palaces 4, 6, 7, 10-11
parliament 6, 7, 17
plants 14, 22, 30-31, 40-41

queens 4, 7, 10, 17, 24, 30

rivers 13, 45
Robin Hood 38-39
rocks 8-9, 14, 26
Romans 4, 32-33

royalty 4, 10, 16, 21, 24, 38

science 18, 30, 36-37
Sherlock Holmes 34-35
statues 28-29, 39, 41, 42-43

towers 4, 6-7, 16-17, 24 44-45
treason 17

United Kingdom 4, 7

wars/conflicts 4, 16, 18, 21, 28-29, 32-33

48